W9-BHL-661

Troubled Treasures: World Heritage Sites

STONEHENGE

Cynthia Kennedy Henzel

ABDO Publishing Company

visit us at
www.abdopublishing.com

Published by ABDO Publishing Company, 8000 West 78th Street, Edina, Minnesota 55439. Copyright © 2011 by Abdo Consulting Group, Inc. International copyrights reserved in all countries. No part of this book may be reproduced in any form without written permission from the publisher. The Checkerboard Library™ is a trademark and logo of ABDO Publishing Company.

Printed in the United States of America, North Mankato, Minnesota.
102010
012011

 PRINTED ON RECYCLED PAPER

Cover Photo: iStockphoto
Interior Photos: Alamy pp. 18, 21; AP Images p. 23; Corbis pp. 19, 25;
    English Heritage Photo Library p. 6; Getty Images pp. 12–13, 17, 28–29;
    iStockphoto pp. 1, 4, 9, 15; Photo Researchers p. 9; Photolibrary pp. 5, 7, 14, 27

Series Coordinator: BreAnn Rumsch
Editors: Megan M. Gunderson, BreAnn Rumsch
Art Direction & Cover Design: Neil Klinepier

Library of Congress Cataloging-in-Publication Data

Henzel, Cynthia Kennedy, 1954-
  Stonehenge / Cynthia Kennedy Henzel.
      p. cm. -- (Troubled treasures--World Heritage sites)
  Includes index.
  ISBN 978-1-61613-567-6
  1. Stonehenge (England)--Juvenile literature. 2. Wiltshire (England)--Antiquities--Juvenile
literature. 3. Megalithic monuments--England--Wiltshire--Juvenile literature. I. Title.
  DA142.H45 2011
  936.2'319--dc22
                                        2010021307

Contents

Long ago, ancient people left behind reminders of their time on England's Salisbury Plain. On this large stretch of land, they built settlements and burial grounds. They also made mysterious structures of earth and stone.

About 10,000 years ago, people dug three holes on the plain. Then, they placed tall pine posts in them. Today, three painted white circles mark where the holes were. We don't know why the holes were made. But we do know they marked a special place.

We know this because Stonehenge was also built there. It was erected more than 4,000 years ago. Stonehenge is most famous for its circle of massive stones. However, the monument consists of circles within circles. Each mysterious circle has its own story.

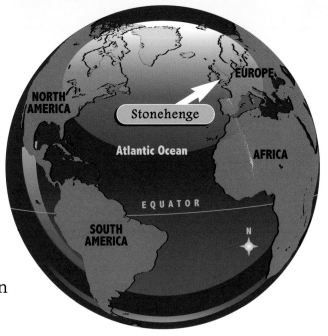

Stonehenge remains one of the world's most impressive stone circles.

There are numerous stone circles in England. One in nearby Avebury is bigger than Stonehenge. Yet Stonehenge is the grandest. **UNESCO** recognized its importance by naming Stonehenge and its surrounding area a World Heritage site. That will help preserve this ancient wonder for years to come.

Many mysterious structures make up Stonehenge. Similar structures can be seen at sites across England. Before stone circles, ancient people built long barrows. They used these rectangular mounds to bury the dead. Most were about 100 feet (30 m) long. Today they look like long, low hills.

Ancient people also built structures called cursus monuments. Each cursus enclosed a rectangular area with earth banks. Around 3100 BC, a large monument known as the Cursus was constructed near Stonehenge. It stretches nearly two miles (3 km) long and more than 100 yards (90 m) wide. Most scientists

Round barrows were often built near one another.

believe it was used for funeral processions.

By about 3000 BC, ancient structures developed into new shapes. People began building barrows that were round. Then, another round structure

Avebury is about 20 miles (30 km) north of Stonehenge. Its henge contains the largest stone circle in Europe.

appeared. People built large, circular banks of earth called henges. Inside a bank lies a deep ditch. Breaks in the ditch allow people to cross to the middle.

One well-known henge was built about two miles (3 km) northeast of Stonehenge. It is called Durrington Walls. Its ditch is almost one mile (1.6 km) around. People built two large wooden buildings inside. Outside, they built many houses.

Research suggests that ancient people began building Stonehenge about 2950 BC. It took about 1,500 years to complete! The work can be grouped into three building stages.

During the first stage, builders made a henge about 320 feet (98 m) across. To dig it, workers used basic tools such as cow bones and deer antlers.

Unlike other henges, the ditch is outside the earth bank. It was made 20 feet (6 m) wide and 5 to 7 feet (1.5 to 2 m) deep. Two openings crossed the ditch. One faced south. A larger one faced northeast.

Inside the henge, the workers dug a ring of 56 holes. Today, these are known as the Aubrey Holes. They did not hold posts or stones. Instead, some held human **remains**.

The second stage likely began by about 2900 BC. Inside and outside the henge, people dug many holes. In these, they erected wooden posts. Today, only empty holes remain. So, we may never know if the posts formed buildings, fences, or other structures.

More to Explore
Around 1600 BC, two more rings of holes were dug. The purpose of these Y and Z holes remains a mystery.

The Three Stages of Stonehenge

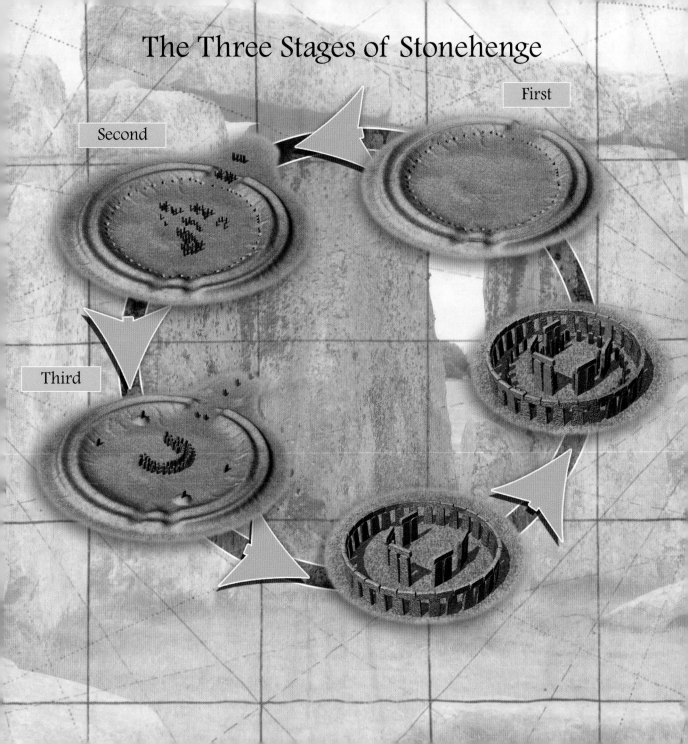

MOVING BLUESTONES

The third building stage of Stonehenge probably began around 2600 BC. This final stage lasted about 1,000 years. The famous stones we see today arrived during this time.

The mysterious bluestones were the first stones to arrive. They are not really blue. Nor are they the largest stones at Stonehenge. Still, people often think the story of these stones is amazing.

The bluestones are not from Salisbury Plain. Instead, they came from the Preseli Mountains in Wales. That is about 250 miles (400 km) away!

These stones were not easy to move, especially over such a long distance. Each weighed about four tons (3.6 t). It most likely took hundreds of people many years to move them.

Scientists believe the workers used ropes to drag the heavy stones to the coast of Wales. There, they put the stones on rafts. The rafts may have traveled along the southern coast of either Wales or England. Next, they would have traveled by river. Finally, the workers had to drag the stones over land.

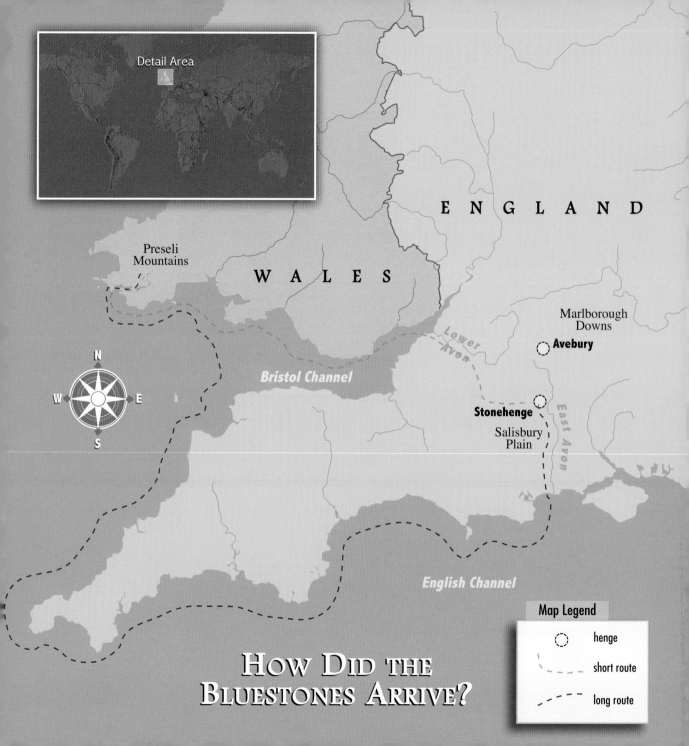

Detail Area

ENGLAND

WALES

Preseli
Mountains

Marlborough
Downs

Avebury

Lower
Avon

Bristol Channel

N

W   E

S

Stonehenge

Salisbury
Plain

East Avon

English Channel

HOW DID THE
BLUESTONES ARRIVE?

Map Legend

○ henge

– – – short route

━ ━ long route

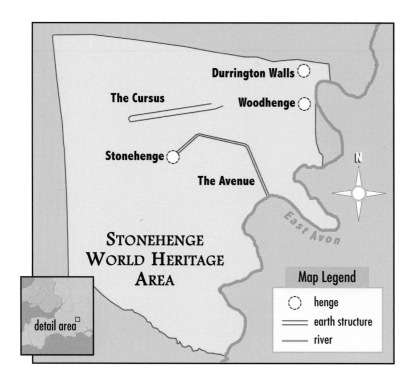

At Stonehenge, the builders dug many holes inside the henge. These formed two half circles, one inside the other. The builders placed bluestones in about 80 of the holes. Many scientists think this design was meant to be two full circles. But, it was never completed.

One bluestone contains shiny specks. It may have been considered special. So, it was set near the middle of the circle. Today, it is known as the Altar Stone.

More to Explore

The bluestones were later moved, and the holes were filled in. Today, the two half circles make up the Q and R holes. The Q holes form the outer arc. The R holes form the inner arc.

The bluestones may look small inside the stone circle. But each stands up to six feet (1.8 m) tall!

One addition to Stonehenge was not a circle. Four large stones were set up outside the bluestones. These Station Stones formed a rectangle.

An imaginary *X* connected the four stones. Its lines crossed at the center of the monument. Scientists believe the Station Stones may have helped builders know where to place other stones.

Today, two Station Stones are left. But, only one remains a full stone. Two low mounds mark where the missing Station Stones once stood. They are known as the North and South barrows.

Later, the builders created a larger monument at Stonehenge. Around 2400 BC, they removed all the bluestones except for the Altar Stone. Next, the builders planned out a bigger circle. It was for large stones called sarsens.

These new stones came from Marlborough Downs, just 20 miles (30 km) away. This was a much shorter journey than the bluestones had taken. However, the sarsens were huge! They stood up to 14 feet (4 m) tall. Most of these stones weighed up to 25 tons (23 t).

Some of the sarsens were meant to stand upright. Others were to become lintels. These would be placed on top of the upright sarsens.

The mortises are visible on this fallen lintel.

This tall sarsen features a well-shaped tenon.

At the site, workers smoothed and shaped the sarsens with **hammerstones**. On the bottom of each lintel, workers pounded out two holes called mortises. At the top of each upright stone, workers made two knobs called tenons. Each mortise fit onto a tenon. This kept the lintels from slipping off the uprights.

Workers also shaped one end of each lintel into a rounded tongue. At the other end, they made a rounded groove. When put together, each tongue and groove kept the stones in place.

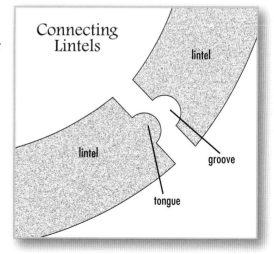

Connecting Lintels

lintel

lintel

groove

tongue

Eventually, the carefully shaped sarsen stones were put in place. First, workers dug a huge hole for each of the 30 upright stones. The holes were sloped on one side.

Hundreds of workers labored to set a single stone in place. Using rollers, they slid a stone into a hole. Slowly, the workers raised the stone using ropes and **levers**. Then, they packed small rocks and dirt into the hole around the stone's base. This held each stone straight.

Next, the workers had to place the lintels on top of the upright sarsens. They used a pole as a lever. After one end of the lintel was raised, they put a log under it. They repeated this process on the other side. Log by log, a platform rose. As it rose, it carried the lintel higher. Finally, the workers could slide the stone into position.

Inside the stone circle, the builders also made five trilithons. Each was like an arch made of two upright sarsens and a lintel. These were the largest stones of the monument. Together, they formed an arc around the Altar Stone. The open end of the arc faced the main entrance to the henge.

More to Explore
Stonehenge is the only stone circle in the world with lintels.

16

The lintels were curved to join together. They crowned the stone circle. When the ring was complete, it stood almost perfectly level.

People once believed the Slaughter Stone was used for sacrifices. However, no evidence supports this idea.

Around 2200 BC, ancient builders made the last major changes to Stonehenge. They added the 80 bluestones back into the monument. About 20 stones made an arc inside the trilithon arc. The remaining 60 made a circle inside the sarsen circle.

Workers also widened the Stonehenge entrance. Then, they erected several large entry stones there. Only one remains. This fallen sarsen is called the Slaughter Stone. It was named for its blood red color, which comes from **iron** in the stone.

Beyond the Slaughter Stone lies the Heel Stone. It sits about 75 feet (23 m) outside the ditch. The Heel Stone is nearly 16 feet (5 m) high. Originally, there were two of these sarsen stones.

The Slaughter and Heel stones sit in an earth structure called the Avenue. Scientists think this pathway might have been used for religious processions. The Avenue is 40 feet (12 m) wide and almost 2 miles (3 km) long. It leads from the East Avon river to Stonehenge's entrance. Earth banks mark the way.

The Heel Stone leans deeply toward the stone circle.

Those who study Stonehenge have many different ideas about its purpose. Some think ancient people used Stonehenge to study the moon.

The positions of the stones may have helped early people track the moon's **cycle**. Some researchers believe the Aubrey Holes may have helped them follow the moon's position.

Others believe Stonehenge was used for tracking the sun. Observers could look out toward the Heel Stone from the henge's center. There, the sun rose over the Heel Stone on the first day of summer. It also set beneath the Heel Stone on the first day of winter.

The stones that can mark the changing moon can also mark the changing sun. This may have happened by accident. Or, perhaps Stonehenge's ancient builders chose this special location on purpose.

Scientists do not know why Stonehenge was built. However,
it is clear the location was sacred to its builders.

Most researchers think Stonehenge was important for more than studying the sky. In fact, they often agree Stonehenge probably served more than one purpose. Many are working to prove this idea.

In 2008, the Stonehenge Riverside Project dated human **remains** at the monument. The results show that Stonehenge was once used as a burial ground.

That same year, another group of scientists began their own research project. They wanted to know why the bluestones were brought so far to Stonehenge. Legend says the **springs** in the Preseli Mountains have healing powers. Perhaps ancient people believed the bluestones found there could heal them.

The team performed a dig inside the stone circle. During their research, they uncovered new information that supports their theory. In the ground, they found flakes from the bluestones. This suggests people chipped off small pieces to keep for good luck.

More to Explore

In 2009, researchers discovered the remains of another stone circle near Stonehenge. They named it Bluehenge for the bluestones it once contained.

The 2008 dig inside the stone circle was the first allowed since 1964.

The scientists also studied human **remains** found around Stonehenge. They learned that many of the people had been sick or injured. Many were also not from the area. This suggests that people traveled far to seek healing at Stonehenge.

By 1500 BC, Stonehenge was abandoned. Over time, people took its stones to make bridges and dams. Today, most of the bluestones are gone. Grazing cattle, burrowing rabbits, and roads caused other stones to fall over.

Eventually, Stonehenge looked like a heap of rocks. Yet, it became a popular place for picnics and sightseeing. During the 1800s, many visitors hammered off pieces of rock to take home. This practice added to the monument's damage.

Luckily, Stonehenge's fate soon changed. In 1915, Sir Cecil Chubb bought the land around Stonehenge. He gave it to England three years later. Then in 1922, the British government began repairing the monument.

Stonehenge quickly became one of England's most popular tourist sites. However, visitors continued to threaten the monument. They often touched and climbed on the stones. More had to be done to protect Stonehenge.

More to Explore

It took much time to move, shape, and raise the stones of Stonehenge. Some scientists have estimated it took workers 2 million hours!

During the 1960s, workers lifted a few toppled stones back into position. They set some in cement to keep them upright.

That Stonehenge Feeling

In 1978, Stonehenge's newest circle was added. It is a roped walkway around the stone circle. People are not allowed inside without special **permission**. This helps protect the ancient monument.

More than 800,000 visitors arrive each year. Tourists like to imagine Stonehenge as ancient people once saw it. However, the Avenue has become barely visible. Instead, a highway cuts a path across Salisbury Plain. Cars cause damaging vibrations and pollution. Noise, crowds, and modern structures all spoil the mysterious feel of Stonehenge.

Keeping Stonehenge safe is a challenge. Today, Stonehenge is managed by English Heritage. This group works to preserve and improve the area around the monument.

English Heritage's next visitor's center will sit farther from the monument. It will offer visitors more education about Stonehenge. English Heritage also supports building a large highway tunnel. It would take traffic underground. These changes will offer future visitors a better experience.

English Heritage hopes moving the highway underground will reconnect the separated parts of the Avenue. The group believes this will help restore an ancient feel to Stonehenge.

SECRETS IN THE STONES

Stonehenge represents 5,000 years of England's early history. The land around the monument whispers secrets of its past.

Scientists still have much to uncover there. For example, another strange monument called Woodhenge was built nearby around 2300 BC. Like Stonehenge, Woodhenge is **aligned** with the sunrise on the first day of summer. Scientists do not know why this wooden structure was built. They wonder if it was somehow connected to Stonehenge.

In 1986, **UNESCO** officials recognized the need to protect Stonehenge for future generations. They named the monument a World Heritage site. The site covers 6,500 acres (2,665 ha) of land. It contains other ancient monuments, including Durrington Walls and Woodhenge.

Researchers hope to someday uncover more of Stonehenge's mysteries. Perhaps the stones are the key to discovering more about this monument's ancient builders. But, Stonehenge does not give up its secrets easily. In the end, this treasure may only reveal a new circle of mysteries to uncover.

Our Valuable World Heritage

Around the globe, UNESCO World Heritage sites represent important civilizations and natural places. Cultural sites include historic buildings, towns, and monuments as well as important archaeological sites. Natural sites contain rare species or natural marvels. Or, they provide important examples of Earth's natural processes. Mixed sites share both cultural and natural elements. World Heritage sites protect and promote these global treasures for future generations.

GLOSSARY

align - to be in line with something.

cycle - a period of time or a complete process that repeats itself.

hammerstone - an ancient tool. It is a rounded stone used as a hammer.

iron - a type of metal that rusts in moist air.

lever - a bar used to pull apart or move something.

permission - formal consent.

remains - a dead body.

spring - a stream of water flowing out of the earth.

UNESCO - United Nations Educational, Scientific, and Cultural Organization. A special office created by the United Nations in 1945. It aims to promote international cooperation in education, science, and culture.

Saying It

Aubrey Holes - AW-bree HOHLZ
Avebury - AYV-buh-ree
lintel - LIHN-tuhl
Marlborough Downs - MAHL-buh-ree DOWNZ
Preseli Mountains - pruh-SEH-lee MOWN-tuhnz
Salisbury Plain - SAWLZ-behr-ee PLAYN
sarsen - SAHR-suhn
trilithon - treye-LIHTH-ahn

Web Sites

To learn more about Stonehenge, visit
ABDO Publishing Company online. Web sites about Stonehenge are
featured on our Book Links page. These links are routinely monitored
and updated to provide the most current information available.
www.abdopublishing.com

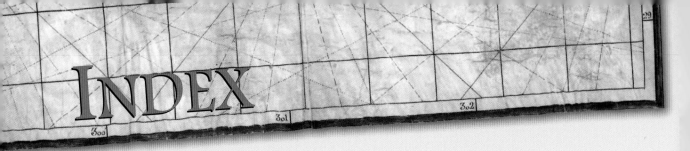

INDEX